FAITHLESS

Jon Klein

BROADWAY PLAY PUBLISHING INC
New York
www.broadwayplaypublishing.com
info@broadwayplaypublishing.com

Cover art by Jennifer Logan, Studio Fuse

First edition: May 2024
I S B N: 979-8-88856-019-8

Book design: Marie Donovan
Page make-up: Adobe InDesign
Typeface: Palatino

FAITHLESS was first developed at PlayFest Santa Barbara in May 2023, directed by Michael Gros.

The World Premiere of FAITHLESS was produced by Maria Gobetti and Evan Bartoletti at The Victory Theatre Center in Burbank, California, running from March to April of 2024. The cast and creative contributors were:

GUS .... John Idakitis
CALVIN .... Jon Sprik
CLAIRE .... Melissa Ortiz
ROSIE...Joseé Gourdine

Director ....Maria Gobetti
Set Designer.. Evan Bartoletti
Lighting Designer... Carol Doehring
Costume Designer.......................................Michael Mullen
Sound Designer .... Noah Andrade
Associate Producer.......................................Erick Marquez
Stage Manager ....Margaret Magula
Assistant Stage Manager............................... Quinn Vasilev
Social media ....Austin Highsmith Garces
Literary Manager..Gail Bryson
Publicity photography..Tim Sullens

CHARACTERS & SETTING

Gus Stanton, *a retired insurance adjustor, around 70*

Claire, *his stepdaughter, a high school teacher, early 30s*

Calvin, *his stepson, a Presbyterian minister, late 30s*

Rosie, *his adopted daughter (person of color preferred), 16*

Time: The present.

*The main setting is a modest and homey study/library in
Gus' house. Books, photo albums, binders, pamphlets on
built-in bookshelves. Nothing too religious or philosophical.
A small fireplace, a desk, a couple of old-fashioned
upholstered chairs, a small loveseat. A few office-related
awards and a college diploma on the walls here and there.
A large picture of his late wife, Carolyn, on display next to
a bible on the mantel (The single exception to the agnostic
environment).*

*In addition, two scenes require a hospital room environment,
which can be simply suggested with a wheeled-on hospital
bed, an IV tower and privacy partition to hide the library.
Probably a folding chair, nothing more is necessary.*

Dedicated to the memory of Tom Ormeny,
for whom this play was originally written.

Scene One

(GUS's study)

(Winter. Saturday night)

(GUS enters the doorway, only to be stopped by a small crash offstage. He turns and yells off.)

GUS: What are you doing, Claire?

CLAIRE: *(OS)* Looking for something to drink!

(CALVIN brushes by GUS in the doorway, carrying some small logs in his arms.)

GUS: Don't bring that stuff in here! It's full of termites.

CALVIN: Oh, be quiet. It's twenty degrees out there. Any termites are long dead. *(He pours the logs into the fireplace and reaches a lighter on the mantel. He struggles to light the fire during the following.)*

GUS: What about snakes? Did you check for snakes?

CALVIN: Good God, Gus. You'd think you lived on swampland.

(CLAIRE yells from off stage.)

CLAIRE: *(OS)* Nothing here! I can't believe it!

(GUS yells back.)

GUS: I told you! *(Back to CALVIN)* This *is* a swampland.

CALVIN: No snakes. I promise you.

GUS: You think I'm kidding. This house was built on a natural spring.

CLAIRE: *(OS)* For heaven's sake. Not one single drop of alcohol in this godforsaken house!

(GUS *yells back.)*

GUS: I already told you that!

CALVIN: *(Also yelling)* He's not supposed to have it, Claire. You know that!

CLAIRE: *(OS)* Not even for guests?

CALVIN: He doesn't have guests!

CLAIRE: *(OS)* Well, what the hell are we supposed to be?

CALVIN: The unwanted stepchildren.

GUS: Unwanted? I'm the one who asked you here!

CALVIN: So you did. I'm still waiting to hear why.

(GUS *yells off again.)*

GUS: Your mother poured all the liquor down the sink! *(To* CALVIN*)* The day I learned about my prostate.

CALVIN: We know, Gus.

GUS: Two years and counting in remission. Knock on wood.

CALVIN: You're really bad at avoiding the subject.

GUS: I'm looking for wood. There's some.

(GUS *reaches over to knock on* CALVIN*'s head.)*

(CALVIN *waves him away.)*

CALVIN: Stop it!

GUS: That won't light, you know.

CALVIN: Just give me a minute.

GUS: We had a storm last night. Everything got covered with a half inch of black ice.

CALVIN: You don't have to tell me. I was just out there. But there was a tarp over the wood.

GUS: Oh yeah.

CALVIN: The tarp was so stiff I could use it for a chair.

GUS: Did you?

CALVIN: Did I what?

GUS: Use it for a chair.

CALVIN: What are you talking about?

GUS: What are *you* talking about?

(CLAIRE *enters, drink in hand.*)

CLAIRE: What are you two talking about?

CALVIN: We have no idea.

GUS: What did you find to drink?

CLAIRE: Cooking sherry. Which is as bad as it sounds. God knows how old it is.

CALVIN: I asked you to fix us some hot coffee.

CLAIRE: It's going, brother dear. I just wanted to find something to put in it. (*She takes a sip.*) This isn't it.

(CALVIN *finally gets a small fire going.*)

CALVIN: Finally. (*He reaches up into the chimney.*)

GUS: What are you doing?

CALVIN: Trying to find the flue.

GUS: That thing hasn't been opened in years. Leave it alone.

CLAIRE: Gus, if he doesn't open the flue, we'll die of asphyxiation.

GUS: Which is why he shouldn't light a fire in the first place. You know what was living over that flue? Raccoons. Animal control came out here and pulled out the babies, one at a time. There were half a dozen of them.

(CALVIN *quickly withdraws his hand.*)

CALVIN: When was this?

GUS: A few years ago. It hasn't been opened since.

CALVIN: It's like the Egyptian plagues around here. What's next, frogs and locusts?

GUS: There's a few mice in the basement. But leave them alone. I've given them names.

CALVIN: Stuff like this is why you're a prime candidate for assisted living.

CLAIRE: He's yanking your chain, Cal. Those raccoons were more like twenty years ago.

CALVIN: You remember it?

CLAIRE: Sure. I was in high school. And mom had a cap put on the chimney. So you don't have to be a baby about it.

(CALVIN *looks at the fireplace, uncertain.*)

CLAIRE: Want me to do it?

CALVIN: I've got it. (*He gingerly opens the flue, which snaps open.*)

CLAIRE: Eee eee eee!

(CALVIN *falls backwards in fright as* CLAIRE *laughs at him.*)

CALVIN: God dammit Claire!

GUS: If you guys are done clowning around, we don't have a lot of time before Rosie comes home.

CLAIRE: Okay, Gus. We're all ears. What's this big announcement all about?

GUS: I can't tell you.

CALVIN: What the—you asked us to come here.

GUS: That's right, I did. I need your help with Rosie. It's serious.

CLAIRE: So you know what it's about?

GUS: Yes.

CLAIRE: But you won't tell us.

GUS: I promised her I wouldn't. But if you're here, and you ask her about it, she'll have to tell her yourself.

CLAIRE: Ask her about what?

GUS: I can't tell you.

CALVIN: Where is she?

GUS: She went ice skating with her friends.

CALVIN: What is this, Gus? Did you bring us here for some kind of intervention?

GUS: Yeah. You could say that.

CALVIN: For what? Drugs?

GUS: Oh no no no. Nothing like that.

CLAIRE: She's pregnant, isn't she? And she's only sixteen.

GUS: Not that either.

CLAIRE: I still bet it's some boy. Am I right?

GUS: I'd rather she tell you herself. I don't want to betray her confidence.

CLAIRE: I bet it's that little creep Andrew. He always picks up her books when she drops them on the way to home room.

CALVIN: How often does that happen?

CLAIRE: At least twice that I've witnessed. And he sits with her at lunch.

CALVIN: Every day?

CLAIRE: At least once a week.

GUS: He just sounds like he's being nice.

CLAIRE: Oh he is. He's probably the nicest kid at Jefferson High. His grades are good, he studies for tests, everyone likes him. I think he's a creep.

GUS: It's not about a boy.

CLAIRE: You would say that even if it was. You've always protected her. You and mom. Poor little adopted Rosie, you both treated her with kid gloves. When I was her age, I was grounded for everything from my skirt length to smoking pot. No sympathy for me. Too bad I wasn't found in a Catholic orphanage in some third world country.

CALVIN: That's an offensive phrase.

CLAIRE: Fine. Developing nation, whatever. I'm just saying kids like Rosie have certain advantages if they make it here to America.

GUS: What's that supposed to mean?

CLAIRE: I don't even know. Don't listen to me. It's the cooking sherry talking.

CALVIN: For God's sake, Claire. Get over these teenage grievances. You're a grown woman, married and divorced.

CLAIRE: What's my divorce got to do with anything?

CALVIN: Divorces, plural.

GUS: Stop it, you two.

CLAIRE: I'd like him to answer my question, Gus. He brings it up every chance he gets. I'd like to hear Calvin give me his oh so authoritarian views on marriage and divorce. Based completely on speculation, certainly not on experience.

CALVIN: Oh, that's effective. Let's impugn the sexuality of a Presbyterian minister.

CLAIRE: Okay, let's.

GUS: Let's not. Can we drop this nonsense and get back to Rosie?

CLAIRE: Sure, by all means, let's ignore whatever is happening with me and talk about her.

GUS: That's why we're here.

CALVIN: *(To* CLAIRE*)* Is something happening with you?

CLAIRE: What?

CALVIN: You just said something's happening with you.

CLAIRE: No I didn't.

CALVIN: You implied it.

CLAIRE: Well, you don't know what the hell you're talking about. Because if you did, you'd know that absolutely *nothing* is happening with me. I'm still teaching the same rotten high school kids, leading the same rotten life of a divorced, childless woman, fending off the same rotten men who think I must be hungry for a quick, uncomplicated fuck, and not very many of them at that, because I'd usually rather stay home and watch Netflix than go out for a drink with the newly divorced dad of one of my students. And Netflix sucks. All of their shows have flashbacks. What's up with that?

(A door slams off stage.)

GUS: She's home. You two clam up and act natural.

*(*CALVIN *and* CLAIRE *take their places and smile broadly at* ROSIE *as she enters the room.* ROSIE *carries ice skates.)*

(She stops to look at them.)

ROSIE: What's wrong?

CLAIRE: Nothing.

CALVIN: We're just glad to see you.

ROSIE: Why?

CLAIRE: How was school today?

ROSIE: You were there. Weren't you?

(CLAIRE *laughs nervously.*)

CLAIRE: That's true!

ROSIE: Why are they being weird, Dad?

GUS: Because they're morons. *(To his stepchildren)* I said natural, damn it! Jesus.

ROSIE: Is something wrong?

GUS: Of course not. How was skating? Did you fall down?

ROSIE: Just a couple of times. Other people were a lot worse.

CLAIRE: Like who? Like Andrew?

ROSIE: No. He's a really good skater.

CLAIRE: I just bet he is. So he was there.

ROSIE: Sure. Most of the class was. We'd been planning it for weeks.

GUS: So it was a fun event.

ROSIE: Yeah. Although that makes it sound weird.

GUS: Not at all. You're a good student, Rosie. You deserve a night of fun.

CLAIRE: Up to a point.

GUS: *Claire. (To* ROSIE*)* Why don't you put your skates in your room, honey? Take off your coat and come down to visit. How about some hot chocolate?

ROSIE: That sounds great.

CALVIN: Do we have any cocoa?

GUS: I don't know, probably. We'll look for it while Rosie gets settled.

ROSIE: Okay. (*She exits.*)

GUS: Damn it, Claire. Don't make me sorry I invited the two of you here.

CALVIN: What did I do?

GUS: You? Nothing. You stood there like a deer in the headlights. Are you two capable of getting your shit together and advising her?

CALVIN: On *what*?

GUS: I can't tell you!

CLAIRE: I know what.

GUS: No you don't. You're way off.

CLAIRE: I don't think so. I'm around these post pubescent kids all day long. The air is absolutely pungent with their runaway pheromones.

GUS: Go get the coffee, Claire. And look for some cocoa. There might be some instant lying around.

CLAIRE: So is the coffee, by the way. I hope you all enjoy six year old Folger's crystals. (*She exits.*)

(CALVIN *sits close to* GUS.)

CALVIN: Okay, Gus. What's this all about, really?

GUS: What does "really" mean? You think I'm hiding something?

CALVIN: You've been admitting it all night.

GUS: Well, only at Rosie's request. She trusts me. And that's important. I want to maintain my relationship with her, especially now that Carolyn's gone. She made me promise that, right before she died.

CALVIN: I understand that, Gus. Claire and I want the same thing.

GUS: With Rosie? Forget it. She barely tolerates the two of you as it is. That's why you can talk to her without repercussions.

CALVIN: She's our sister, you know.

GUS: Stepsister. That's not the same. Your mom and I wanted a child of our own.

CALVIN: Is that what you call her?

GUS: Sure. Your mother and I patiently waited for any sign of grandchildren from you and your sister.

CALVIN: I was just out of divinity school, Gus. And Claire was still in college.

GUS: That's right. We realized the futility of waiting on you two. So your mother and I decided to have a kid of our own.

CALVIN: Gus—

GUS: Rosie and I have a closer relationship. We're connected by blood.

CALVIN: No you're not. You and mom adopted her. Or have you forgotten?

GUS: No, I haven't forgotten. And quit implying that I have dementia. When I get dementia you'll know it, believe me. You won't have to wonder.

CALVIN: I'm just saying, adoption is hardly a blood connection.

GUS: The hell it's not. The first time I picked her up in that orphanage, she bit me. And drew blood. That's what I'm talking about.

CALVIN: Not the same thing.

GUS: It was like a love nip from a puppy. She didn't know how to express her glee that we might rescue her from those third world missionaries. I took it as a sign that she was preordained to be our child. We were bonded for life.

CALVIN: Mom said she wanted three of them, not just Rosie.

GUS: Your mother was big hearted. But somewhat removed from reality.

(ROSIE *enters.*)

ROSIE: You all talking about Mom?

GUS: CALVIN:
No.   Yes.

CALVIN: I was telling your Dad it's probably time to take the Christmas wreath out of the cemetary. I did a funeral there last week and other people are setting up lilies for Easter.

GUS: There's no hurry.

CALVIN: Says the man who has a deflated Santa on his roof.

GUS: You wanna climb up there, be my guest.

ROSIE: Christmas was Mom's favorite holiday.

CALVIN: That it was.

GUS: Indeed.

ROSIE: I wish she could have—

(CLAIRE *enters with a tray of coffee cups, cream and sugar.*)

CLAIRE: Here we go. No hot chocolate, sorry. But tell you what. Cocoa is basically just coffee with sugar and milk. So try adding that in and it will taste pretty similar.

ROSIE: Thanks. (*She begins to put a lot of sugar in her cup.*)

GUS: She's too young for coffee.

ROSIE: Please, Dad. My friends all practically live at the Starbucks a block from school.

CLAIRE: That's true, I've seen them there when they cut their classes.

ROSIE: This is great, thanks. *(She takes a sip, then looks up at everyone warily.)* Why are you all staring at me?

CLAIRE: All right. Let's cut to the chase.

GUS: Claire—

CALVIN: This is not the way to—

CLAIRE: Who did it to you?

(Pause)

ROSIE: Excuse me?

CLAIRE: It's that little creep Andrew, isn't it? The perfect skater.

ROSIE: What are you—

CALVIN: Claire, this is by no means—

CLAIRE: Is it someone else? Because I promise you this. I may be hopped up on expired caffeine and cooking sherry, but I will happily take it upon myself to cut his balls off. Just give me a name.

GUS: Claire, shut up!

CLAIRE: But I—

GUS: Sit there with your mouth shut for the next five minutes. Or else I'll ask you to leave.

(Pause. CLAIRE *defiantly takes a chair and sits down.)*

*(*ROSIE *turns to* GUS.*)*

ROSIE: You told them, didn't you?

GUS: Honey, no, scout's honor, I promise I didn't tell them a thing.

ROSIE: What is this scout's honor? You mean like a merit badge?

CALVIN: He's saying he didn't break your confidence. And he didn't. But Gus suggested that you might have something to share with us. If you want to.

(ROSIE *turns to* GUS.)

ROSIE: You asked them here to—

GUS: Yes. I think it's best to discuss this out in the open.

ROSIE: But I don't want to. I told you that.

GUS: It's not healthy to keep something like this a secret from your family.

CALVIN: Oh, I think I know what's going on.

ROSIE: Believe me, you don't.

CALVIN: Rosie, I counsel young people all the time about questions regarding their sexual orientation.

CLAIRE: God help them.

GUS: Just let her talk, for God's sake.

ROSIE: That's not it, Calvin.

CALVIN: Don't be embarassed. These feelings can be very fluid. And can take a while to sort out.

ROSIE: Oh my God.

GUS: Shut up, Calvin.

CALVIN: Okay, okay. Just know we're your family and we're behind whatever you decide.

CLAIRE: It's not a decision, Minister. Quit talking like you're from the seventies.

CALVIN: Says the woman who refers to third world countries.

ROSIE: Please stop, I beg you.

CALVIN: We just want you to feel free to talk to us. About anything.

ROSIE: Not about this.

CLAIRE: Yes, about anything. Everyone here loves you and nothing you can ever do will prevent that.

GUS: Exactly. Well said.

CLAIRE: Thank you.

CALVIN: For a change.

ROSIE: Just stop talking. I'll tell you if you stop talking.

CLAIRE: We won't say another word. We're here to listen, not to lecture. We don't care what it is, we'll be completely—

GUS: Claire!

CLAIRE: Sorry. Proceed.

(ROSIE *takes a long sip of coffee, preparing herself. She puts the cup down.)*

ROSIE: Actually…this *does* involve a decision.

CALVIN: Okay.

CLAIRE: Shhh.

ROSIE: But not what you think. *(Pause. With determination)* I've decided I want to become a nun.

(Long pause)

(CALVIN *and* CLAIRE *stare at* ROSIE. GUS *shakes his head.)*

CALVIN: Can you repeat that?

ROSIE: A nun.

CALVIN: As in…

ROSIE: A Catholic nun. I want to become one.

(Another pause)

CLAIRE: Are you sure you're not pregnant?

ROSIE: Yes, I'm sure.

CLAIRE: Because that would be better.

GUS: That's enough, Claire.

ROSIE: Well, this has been really helpful, you guys. *(She stands up to leave.)*

CALVIN: Don't listen to them, Rosie. Just tell us how this all came about. If you would.

*(*ROSIE *hesitates, then sits again.)*

ROSIE: Well, it actually started in Claire's class.

CLAIRE: What? Comparative Religion?

ROSIE: It started me thinking.

CLAIRE: That class deals with fifteen different religions. A different one every week. I take great pains not to advocate any one over the other.

ROSIE: I know. You are very good about that.

CLAIRE: For God's sake, your class presentation was on the Rosicrucians! How did you come to land on Catholicism?

ROSIE: I don't know. It just appealed to me.

CLAIRE: You can't just try on religions like you're trying on clothes at The Gap.

CALVIN: Look who's talking.

GUS: If you want my opinion—

ROSIE: You've made your opinion very clear already, Dad. You call religion a fairy tale.

GUS: Not all of it. To be fair, I believe that Jesus was probably a real person. Who tried to convince people to lead better lives and was tortured and killed for his troubles. I don't diminish his importance. That's huge. Historically, culturally, it's inescapable.

ROSIE: So why try?

GUS: It's all the magic tricks that offend me. Water into wine, feeding the multitudes, raising the dead, all that nonsense. He might as well have been pulling rabbits out of hats. Or cutting his lovely assistant in half.

CLAIRE: I doubt if Mary Magdalene would have stood for that.

GUS: And the so-called miracle of Sunday mass, eating his body and drinking his blood once a week, like an appetizer to Sunday Brunch. The Catholics take it literally, you know. It's grotesque.

ROSIE: I don't see it that way.

GUS: Well, you should. How's it any better than turning into a swan, or riding a flying horse, or snakes in some woman's hair that will freeze you at thirty paces? All that mythical stuff is fun when you're a child, but there comes a time when you must put away childish things.

CALVIN: Said Paul the Apostle.

GUS: I don't deny the Bible can offer good lessons. But the word of God? Give me a break.

ROSIE: I want to believe it. I do believe it.

CLAIRE: Maybe you were right the first time.

CALVIN: And that's fine, Rosie. You were inspired by your studies. I commend you for that.

ROSIE: That's right. Other people are inspired to be doctors. Or lawyers, or actors, or bakers. Why can't I be inspired to be a nun?

CLAIRE: Because, my sweet confused stepsister, of all the antifeminist, masochistic, patriarchal professions you could choose, being the bride of Christ is probably at the top of the list.

ROSIE: That's just a saying. You don't actually marry anyone. Ever.

CLAIRE: And you like the sound of that?

Rosie: Since when has marriage been a big success for you?

Calvin: Touche.

Claire: Fine. I've never told you to follow my example. I'm a lousy role model and I know it. But just because I've made a hash of my personal life doesn't mean you'll do the same. You'll do better when your time comes, I know it.

Rosie: I think this *is* my time.

Calvin: Look, Rosie. No one is here to talk you out of what you want.

Claire: I am.

Gus: Me too.

Calvin: Let's be constructive, folks. Rosie—I wonder if it would behoove you to do a little research on what it involves to become a nun. I suspect you have an idealized vision of what it involves.

Claire: Yeah, it's not all singing and escaping Nazis.

Rosie: I've done research.

Calvin: Okay. Like what?

Rosie: I made an appointment and visited The Little Sisters of the Poor.

Claire: Damn it. We did a Christmas drive for them last year. I begged the Principal not to let them into the building. They're as bad as the Hare Krishnas.

Calvin: Is that who you want to join?

Rosie: Not necessarily. But I like the idea of joining an order that serves others like the homeless or the sick.

Calvin: Commendable.

Claire: Depressing.

GUS: Pointless. There will always be poor people. We can't change that. Who said that, someone famous I think.

(They give GUS *a look.)*

GUS: Ah shoot. It was Jesus, wasn't it?

CALVIN: Don't pay them any attention, I'm listening. And I respect your interest in religion. Though not necessarily that one. What did the Sisters tell you?

ROSIE: They said I should probably still go to college.

CLAIRE: Thank God for that.

ROSIE: But they also said I should sign up with a vocation director. And do weekend retreats. I found a great app called VocationMatch.com.

CLAIRE: What, like Tinder for nuns?

ROSIE: Sort of. After college, I can pick a convent, live with them and be a pre-candidate. That usually takes a couple of years. Then I become a novice for one to two years. I have to study and work along with the other sisters.

CLAIRE: So far that's four years. And you're still an intern.

ROSIE: Maybe longer. Then I take my first vows, which I do every year for the next five to nine years.

GUS: Vows of what?

ROSIE: Oh, you know, chastity, poverty, obedience, that kind of thing.

CLAIRE: Jesus Christ.

ROSIE: That's another vow. And I'll probably have to cut my hair short. I get a new name, and a habit if I want to wear one. I think I will. Then I take my final vows. And I get a ring. I'm in.

CLAIRE: So we're talking ten years or so.

GUS: Okay. What's the pay?

ROSIE: Oh Dad, I already said I take a vow of poverty. We don't get paid. We just have room and board supplied by the convent.

CLAIRE: So far it sounds like the first four-fifths of a Dickens novel. With no last chapter.

ROSIE: Becoming a nun is the last chapter.

CALVIN: Okay, clearly you know what you're in for. But why?

CLAIRE: Yes, why would you willingly subject yourself to a life of hardship and loneliness?

ROSIE: I don't know if I can explain it. I just know that I've been called.

GUS: Are you hearing voices?

ROSIE: Sort of. Except it's my own voice. Telling me I need to devote myself to others.

CLAIRE: But that's so…limiting!

ROSIE: I think it could be freeing.

CLAIRE: Rosie. Even you must know the inequity. Priests get to play golf, have poker parties and scout for little boys if they're so inclined.

CALVIN: That's not—

CLAIRE: While nuns get to pray the rosary and eat soup in silence with the Mother Superior.

CALVIN: That's an exaggeration.

ROSIE: No, I know what she means. But I think that can change in time.

CLAIRE: Really? After two thousand years of institutiional suppression? Good luck with that.

CALVIN: Let's talk about something else. Have you really thought about all the things you'll be giving up?

GUS: I tried to tell her. She wouldn't listen.

ROSIE: That's not true, Dad. I listened to every word you said. Parties. Dating. Sex. Money.

GUS: Fun.

CLAIRE: And you don't want any of that? Why not? Maybe the pressure of a social life is too hard for you.

ROSIE: I had fun tonight. I have no problem with it.

CLAIRE: I wonder.

GUS: What about a career? Professional accomplishment. It meant a lot to me. Look around these walls. I was good at my job, and that gave me a lot of satisfaction.

ROSIE: Good for you, Dad.

GUS: Not that I want you to be a claims adjuster.

CLAIRE: God no. Let's get back to the fun stuff.

ROSIE: Look. I understand what you all are saying. It's not like I haven't thought about it. I have.

GUS: Okay then.

ROSIE: And I'm not saying it's wrong to want things. I'm just saying—how do I put this—there's nothing consistent in the secular world.

GUS: Where'd you hear that? That sounds like brainwash talk.

CLAIRE: More like Tik Tok talk.

GUS: She doesn't even sound like a teenager.

CLAIRE: You don't know how teenagers talk, Gus.

ROSIE: That's for sure.

CLAIRE: I hear them talk about this stuff every day at the high school. They think the things we strived for are bullshit.

GUS: Like what?

CLAIRE: Like everything. Love, sex, money, homes, careers. You name it. If we ever wanted it, they want no part of it.

GUS: Why not?

CLAIRE: Because they see what it did to us. And they see how we fucked up our lives.

GUS: I beg to differ. I didn't—using a different word, since there's a child in the room—

ROSIE: I'm not a child.

GUS: I didn't screw up my life. Or yours. How about you, Calvin?

CLAIRE: Yeah, how about you, Calvin?

CALVIN: I'm not taking that bait, Claire. Get back to your point.

CLAIRE: My point is, times have changed, that's all. It wasn't too hard for us to find jobs and places to live and life partners without too much effort. But kids today have trouble seeing those things in their future. They're looking into a big thick fog. When I think about it, I'm not surprised that Rosie is drawn to a way of life where everything is laid out for her so neatly. She'd be taken care of. Like she was in the orphanage.

ROSIE: That's not fair.

GUS: I don't understand any of this.

CLAIRE: It's called authoritarianism. Young people crave it.

CALVIN: Claire may have a point. I read an article about this last week. A new poll says twenty-five percent of young people have decided they don't like Democracy.

ROSIE: Hello. Remember me? Suddenly I'm not even in the room.

CALVIN: Sorry. We got off track.

ROSIE: That's one way to put it. Great talk, guys. Very supportive. *(She stands to go.)*

GUS: Don't go, honey.

ROSIE: Thanks for listening. With open minds. Using a certain word even though there's a *child* in the room, you can all go fuck yourselves. *(She heads out the door.)*

CLAIRE: We're sorry. Please stay.

CALVIN: She doesn't have to. Rosie is right.

(ROSIE *stops and turns. Pause)*

ROSIE: I am?

CALVIN: Sure you are. Who are we to tell you what to believe about anything? Our whole family is steeped in the brine of religious blunders.

GUS: Not me.

CALVIN: You most of all. Trying to get our mom to deny her own faith.

GUS: I did no such thing.

CALVIN: You knew she was a dedicated Presbyterian. To the point of naming me after the head of the Protestant Reformation—Calvin. You think it's sheer coincidence I became a minister? She wanted it more than anything. Especially after our own Dad suddenly died.

ROSIE: Didn't you want to be a minister?

CALVIN: Not necessarily. But it gave her comfort. Only to have Gus make her leave the church when she married him . An avowed atheist.

GUS: Although I am the only baptized Catholic in this room. I just couldn't take all that crap by the time I was Rosie's age. No offense, Rosie.

ROSIE: Seriously?

GUS: *(To* CALVIN*)* And you're wrong. I never forced your mom to quit anything. She only came there to watch you preach. See her son at work.

CALVIN: But you kept telling her it was all nonsense.

GUS: And she agreed. She had more sense than that.

CLAIRE: Than what?

GUS: Than God.

CALVIN: Wow. First of all, you're full of shit. Secondly, does everyone see why Rosie might like a little spiritual certainty?

CLAIRE: Tell me about it. I've been searching for something to believe in my whole life. I got a Masters in Religious Studies, hoping I'd find something that made sense if I looked hard enough. I even married a Buddhist. His idea of spiritual meditation was drinking beer and watching ESPN. So I got rid of him and married a rabbi. Who decided to have an affair with an Episcopalian heiress. His religious goal was apparently to join a country club.

CALVIN: Anyway. Rosie. You see how you might have been negatively influenced. We're largely to blame. When you were adopted, you came home to a family that loved you, but also one that—let's face it—is pretty fraught with religious strife and confusion. No wonder you're attracted to a system where faith equals fact.

CLAIRE: And admit it, you probably do have some subconscious memories of that Catholic orphanage, and how nice those nuns were to you when you were a baby. So you're wondering what it would be like to be one yourself.

ROSIE: Is that so wrong?

GUS: Of course not, honey.

CLAIRE: It's only natural. That's what we're saying.

CALVIN: Look. We just want you to think about it. That's all.

GUS: You've got plenty of time. All the time in the world.

ROSIE: Okay. I guess you're right about that.

CLAIRE: Thank God. So to speak.

CALVIN: Did we help at all?

ROSIE: I suppose..

CALVIN: Then we'll leave it at that. Okay, everybody?

GUS: Okay.

CLAIRE: Okay. Now I want a drink. An actual drink. I'm going to the liquor store down the street.

GUS: I wouldn't mind a splash of brandy.

CALVIN: Gus—

GUS: To warm me up on a cold night. What do you say, Rosie? Okay with you?

ROSIE: I don't care either way. I'm not old enough to drink.

CLAIRE: Sure you are. How about a hard lemonade?

ROSIE: What's that?

CLAIRE: Something sweet that might also give you a little buzz.

ROSIE: Really? That would be okay?

CLAIRE: Gus?

GUS: Sure. Why not? You better try everything you can until they take it away from you.

CALVIN: Not everything.

GUS: Right. Within reason.

CLAIRE: I'll walk there and be right back.

GUS: You'll do no such thing. You'll slip and break your spine.

CLAIRE: Rosie, come with me. You can take my arm and we'll slide there together.

GUS: Good idea. Go with her.

ROSIE: Okay, I'll get my coat. *(She runs out.)*

GUS: This didn't exactly go the way I hoped.

CALVIN: Give her time, Gus.

CLAIRE: Yeah, don't be stupid. If you keep telling her not to do it you'll probably push her right into it.

GUS: Yeah. I can see that.

CLAIRE: Too bad she wasn't pregnant. I had a plan for that.

CALVIN: Sure you don't want me to drive?

CLAIRE: No, let me bond with her on the walk. She'll feel better.

GUS: Absolutely.

(ROSIE returns, wearing her own coat and carrying CLAIRE's.)

ROSIE: Ready.

CLAIRE: Let's see, brandy, soft drink with a kick, *(Pointing to herself)* bourbon and—?

CALVIN: I'll stick with coffee.

CLAIRE: Irish?

CALVIN: Okay.

CLAIRE: There's always Mom's bible if you need reading material. Otherwise you'll have to talk to each other.

CALVIN: I think we'll be fine.

CLAIRE: That would be a first.

ROSIE: Let's go, Claire.

(CLAIRE *and* ROSIE *leave.*)

(*Pause.* CALVIN *stokes the fire.*)

GUS: I wish Carolyn could have been here for this.

CALVIN: Me too.

GUS: She would have known how to handle it.

CALVIN: Not necessarily.

GUS: No doubt about it. She had the patience. And the tenderness. And she would have gently talked her out of it.

CALVIN: She's young, Gus. She'll come around.

GUS: I hope so. I want her to be happy. But I don't want her to believe in this nonsense.

CALVIN: Like Mom did, I suppose.

GUS: Hey. I never kept her from going to your church. She wanted to see her son preach. Every Sunday. Even during Covid. No matter what the cost.

(*Pause.* CALVIN *turns to* GUS, *his expression changed.*)

CALVIN: What does that mean?

GUS: Nothing.

CALVIN: Oh it means something all right. Why don't you spit it out?

GUS: Never mind.

(The sound of tires squealing at a distance outside. A distant scream is heard.

GUS: You don't think—

CALVIN: I don't know.

GUS: Help me up.

(CALVIN *helps* GUS *get to his feet, and they both exit.*)

Scene Two

(*A hospital room*)

(*Early Sunday morning.*)

(CLAIRE *is in a hospital bed, with a partition nearby. She has a large bandage on her head, and is hooked up to an IV tower.*)

(*She is newly awake when lights come up, looking around her with consternation, and with confusion at the drip leading to her wrist. She tries to sit up but falls back, dizzy.*)

(GUS *quickly enters, followed by* ROSIE *and* CALVIN.)

GUS: Whoa, whoa, where are you going?

CLAIRE: Gus?

GUS: Yes, yes, it's your stepfather Gus, remember me?

CLAIRE: What do you mean, remember you? Have you been away?

GUS: I've been here right here all night. Just left for a minute to fetch these two. Looked like you were starting to come around.

CALVIN: Let me through. Claire. Do you know who I am?

CLAIRE: Martin Luther.

CALVIN: Who are you?

CLAIRE: Marie Antoinette.

CALVIN: How many fingers am I holding up?

CLAIRE: Thirteen.

(CALVIN *turns to the others.*)

CALVIN: She seems okay.

CLAIRE: I think I already went through that with somebody.

CALVIN: One more test. *(He turns back to her.)* Remember me, your old pal Hunk? And me, Hickory? You couldn't forget my face, could you?

GUS: What the hell are you doing, Calvin?

ROSIE: I know what he's doing. It's her favorite movie.

CLAIRE: The Wizard of Oz.

CALVIN: There, see? She's gonna be just fine.

CLAIRE: I don't feel just fine.

(ROSIE comes forward.)

ROSIE: Hi Claire. It's Rosie.

CLAIRE: I can see that, babe.

ROSIE: I'm so glad you're better. I've been praying for you.

CLAIRE: Uh oh. I don't like the sound of that.

CALVIN: You're going to have a headache for a while, sis. Maybe a few days. Want some Tylenol? I can get the nurse.

CLAIRE: What I want is a stiff drink.

GUS: Not yet, honey.

CLAIRE: Anything else I should know?

CALVIN: Not much. Just that we'll need to watch you for a while. Rosie has offered to stay with you, to wake you up every few hours. Just to be sure.

CLAIRE: Sure of what?

(CALVIN looks at GUS and ROSIE.)

GUS: Don't look at us. Tell her.

CALVIN: Claire. You were in and out of consciousness. We thought…for a while…we thought we might lose you.

GUS: We don't want you slipping away again.

CLAIRE: Slipping…I think I remember slipping.

ROSIE: That's right, you did. Out on Bashford Lane. Down from Dad's house. It was scary.

CLAIRE: Was there…a car? Did it hit me?

CALVIN: It never touched you. But it slid sideways on the ice, and you ran from it. Right, Rosie? She was there.

ROSIE: You tried to turn and run away, but you fell and hit your head on the sidewalk.

GUS: We heard Rosie scream.

CALVIN: It was touch and go for a while.

CLAIRE: What a strange phrase. Touch. And go. Go where?

GUS: Nowhere.

ROSIE: Thank God.

CLAIRE: Wait a minute. Are you saying…I was in a coma?

CALVIN:	GUS:
Sort of.	Not at all.

GUS glares at CALVIN.

GUS: In and out, like we've been saying.

CLAIRE: So they say I have a con…what's it called? I can't think of the word. My head hurts.

CALVIN: A concussion. Possibly a contusion. Which is a little more serious, like a bruise on the brain. They gave you a CT scan and didn't find any bleeding. So it's just a minor brain trauma.

CLAIRE: Minor brain trauma. That seems like an oxen …oxy… *(She rubs her forehead.)*

CALVIN: Oxymoron.

GUS: Not at all. There's nothing to worry about.

CLAIRE: What about Rosie? She looks worried.

GUS: Stop that, Rosie.

(ROSIE *breaks into tears and leaves the room.)*

CALVIN: Way to go, Gus.

GUS: Well, she's too emotional.

CALVIN: Probably back to the chapel. She feels better there.

CLAIRE: You all are not giving me confidence.

CALVIN: Believe us, you're fine. They're going to release you as soon as the doctor visits you in the morning.

CLAIRE: The morning? What time is it?

GUS: About four AM on Sunday. We'd all been at my house, talking about Rosie. Remember? Rosie's announcement?

CLAIRE: Oh yeah. I was hoping that was a dream.

GUS: No such luck.

CALVIN: Did you have dreams?

CLAIRE: I'm…not sure. I remember being somewhere else.

CALVIN: Dream activity is a good sign. Your brain was functioning.

CLAIRE: But it didn't feel like a dream. How long was I out?

GUS: Like we're telling you. You were never completely out. You opened your eyes and tried to talk. Then you went back to sleep.

CLAIRE: How long?

CALVIN: About five hours.

CLAIRE: I don't remember.

GUS: You were unconscious when the ambulance arrived. Rosie and I rode with you, and Calvin drove right behind. They took you right into X-Ray.

CLAIRE: And you all stayed?

GUS: We never left the hospital. Rosie and Calvin went to the chapel.

CALVIN: And Gus went to the cafeteria.

CLAIRE: Really?

GUS: That's not the way it sounds. I bought some coffee and came back to the emergency room until they admitted you. They said they saw no signs of bleeding, so you would probably come around in an hour or so.

CALVIN: You took longer, but that's okay.

(ROSIE *returns.*)

ROSIE: I'm sorry. I'm such a baby sometimes.

(GUS *goes to* ROSIE *and hugs her.*)

GUS: My fault, Rosie.

CALVIN: We're all stressed out.

CLAIRE: Interesting how nobody hugs the person in the hospital bed.

(*They all rush toward her, but retreat when she picks up a plastic utensil from her tray.*)

CLAIRE: Back off! Don't make me use this spork!

CALVIN: See? She's back to normal.

CLAIRE: Besides, I don't want you ripping out my IV. What are they feeding me, anyway?

GUS: They told us, but I can't—

CALVIN: I looked it up. It's called Mannitol. Some kind of artificial sweetener—

CLAIRE: They think I'm *fat*?

CALVIN: No. It's also used to pull water from the cranium in the event of cerebral edema.

CLAIRE: Thank you, Doctor.

CALVIN: No need to be snide. I'm just trying to stay informed. Should I send for the nurse?

CLAIRE: I think I just want some quiet now. Gus, you and Rosie can go. No need for all of you to stay. Calvin can hang out awhile. He can read me more medical websites until I finally fall asleep and he clangs a cymbal.

ROSIE: That was my job.

CLAIRE: You get some sleep while you can. Then you can take over when they send me home. Come here. I'll take a hug from the girl who prayed for me.

(ROSIE *hugs* CLAIRE *in the bed.*)

CLAIRE: Thank you, sis. You know I'll always love you, right? Even if you do want to dress like a penguin.

ROSIE: I know.

CLAIRE: Did God say anything to you tonight? When you pled my case?

ROSIE: I didn't talk to God. I talked to Jesus.

CLAIRE: Uh-oh. Catholics don't make that distinction, you know.

ROSIE: I can't talk to God. His pictures scare me. He always looks like he's about to smite somebody.

CLAIRE: Ah yes. I know what you mean. While Jesus looks like boyfriend material.

(ROSIE *laughs, embarassed.*)

ROSIE: Stop it!

CLAIRE: Better Him than Andrew, I say.

GUS: You sure you want us to go?

CLAIRE: Please.

CALVIN: I'll call you guys when the doctor releases her.

GUS: Okay. Thanks.

(GUS *walks over to* CLAIRE *and kisses her forehead.*)

CLAIRE: Ow.

GUS: Oh stop. I'm so glad everything turned out okay. I really am.

CLAIRE: Glad you think so, Gus. Like Mom used to say, consider the alternative.

ROSIE: See you soon!

(*They exit.*)

CALVIN: Okay, I assume you want some stuff from home. I put your purse in the cabinet, but you'll want some clothes. Yours got pretty wet and muddy when you took a header on Bashford Lane.

CLAIRE: In a minute. I want to ask you something.

CALVIN: Shoot.

CLAIRE: I may have some trouble finding the right words.

CALVIN: That's okay. We can talk about it later.

CLAIRE: No, let's talk about it now, damn it! Can't you just sit there and fucking *listen* for a change?

(CALVIN *is stunned into silence.*)

CLAIRE: Thank you. Sorry about that.

CALVIN: That's okay. They said there might be some sudden moments of rage.

CLAIRE: God damn it, shut up! This is important!

(CALVIN *begins to say something, then stops.)*

CLAIRE: Please, Calvin. I don't want to yell at you. I want your honest feedback. As my brother.

CALVIN: You bet.

CLAIRE: And a minister.

(Pause)

CALVIN: Really?

CLAIRE: You heard me.

CALVIN: This is the first time you've ever asked me for spiritual advice. Ever.

CLAIRE: This is the first time I almost died.

CALVIN: Oh, well, you don't have to think about that now.

CLAIRE: I am thinking about it. Like it or not. I think that's pretty understandable, don't you?

CALVIN: Well, if you—

CLAIRE: That was not actually a question. Despite my inflection.

CALVIN: Okay.

CLAIRE: So. According to you, I was…gone.

CALVIN: Not completely. You were—

CLAIRE: In and out. So I heard. What I want to know is…when I was out…where did I go?

CALVIN: You didn't go anywhere. We might have moved you if they didn't give you a private room. But they're not that busy tonight.

CLAIRE: Let me try again. I know my body remained here. Physically. But I'm pretty sure *I* went somewhere else.

CALVIN: What do you mean?

CLAIRE: I went to…some other place.

CALVIN: You mean mentally?

CLAIRE: Sure. If you wanna put it that way.

CALVIN: So where did you go?

CLAIRE: That's what I'd like to know.

CALVIN: Are you talking about a dream?

CLAIRE: No. I know what dreams are like. This definitely wasn't a dream.

CALVIN: How do you know?

CLAIRE: This was real. It felt more real than me talking to you.

CALVIN: You always say talking to me is unreal.

CLAIRE: I mean this—all of this—being alive—does not feel real.

CALVIN: I see.

CLAIRE: You do?

CALVIN: Sure. You probably did have a contusion. The nurse said it wouldn't be unusual to have a few days of confusion. Hey, that rhymes with contusion. Maybe we can write a song together, what do you think?

CLAIRE: I don't want to write a song, Calvin. I want you to stop talking to me like I'm a child, and try to listen to what I'm trying to tell you. I went somewhere. Somewhere else. Somewhere other than here. I was there. Actually there. Not here. Do you understand me yet?

CALVIN: Are you saying…you went somewhere?

CLAIRE: For God's sake—

CALVIN: Okay, okay. Are you talking about … the afterlife?

CLAIRE: I don't know if was the afterlife. All I know is that it was…some other life. Besides this one.

CALVIN: You mean Heaven?

CLAIRE: I didn't see any road signs, Calvin. Nothing that said, "Welcome to Heaven, Population a hundred billion, Lions Club Bingo, Thursday nights."

CALVIN: What did you see? Could you tell anything about where you were?

CLAIRE: Yes. It felt like I'd been there before.

CALVIN: You mean in this life? Or a previous life?

CLAIRE: This life.

CALVIN: Okay, so let's recount the memorable places you've been. Paris? New York? The Grand Canyon? Disneyland? Please don't say Disneyland.

CLAIRE: It was like…a big field.

CALVIN: What kind of field?

CLAIRE: A field of tall grass, as far as the eye could see. Not flat land, though. Rolling hills. And there was a gentle wind, which I could hear blowing through the grass.

CALVIN: That's it? Grass?

CLAIRE: That's it.

CALVIN: No people?

CLAIRE: No.

CALVIN: Or people with wings?

CLAIRE: Are you really this stupid or are you fucking with me?

CALVIN: Sorry.

CLAIRE: I was alone. Except…

CALVIN: Yes?

CLAIRE: There were other things there. Things that moved, in the distance.

CALVIN: What kind of things?

CLAIRE: I don't know. Big black, round things. I couldn't make them out in any detail. But they were moving.

CALVIN: Were they bugs?

CLAIRE: What?

CALVIN: Giant bugs?

CLAIRE: No! Nothing like that. They didn't frighten me in the least. As a matter of fact, I was happy to see them.

CALVIN: Why?

CLAIRE: I don't know. The whole place just gave me a feeling of…inner peace. Like I was welcome.
And I wanted to stay.

CALVIN: In a field of grass.

CLAIRE: It was beautiful. Green and lush, swaying like waves on the ocean. And I think it was dawn. The sky was red and purple.

CALVIN: Like it was on fire?

CLAIRE: No, like it was *dawn*. Or sundown. It was majestic.

CALVIN: No long tunnel.

CLAIRE: No.

CALVIN: With a bright light at the end.

CLAIRE: Nothing like that.

CALVIN: And no one was there.

CLAIRE: No.

CALVIN: And no one spoke to you.

CLAIRE: No.

CALVIN: Any refreshments?

CLAIRE: *Calvin.*

CALVIN: Just grass.

CLAIRE: That's right.

CALVIN: So based on your observations… Heaven is apparently a less interesting version of the least interesting place on earth.

CLAIRE: I never called it Heaven.

CALVIN: The afterlife, then.

CLAIRE: I'm not calling it that either. I'm calling it an… alternative existence.

CALVIN: A place where you stand around in the grass like a cow. Waiting for something to happen.

CLAIRE: It wasn't a place to wait. It was a place to be in the moment.

CALVIN: For how long?

CLAIRE: I don't know.

CALVIN: So…it's not heaven.

CLAIRE: Not the way you think of it. No.

CALVIN: It's some gigantic agrarian holding pen.

CLAIRE: Look. All I know is that I felt I was in a place of total peace and utter calmness, with no anxiety, and no sense of anything that has to be done by a certain time. Because there was no time.

CALVIN: Eternity still has time. It means forever.

CLAIRE: I never said I would be there forever. I just said I was there.

CALVIN: Alright. You can cut out the act now. It's getting annoying.

CLAIRE: I'm not acting.

CALVIN: Then you're having some kind of post-concussive delusion. Either way, it's not worth repeating.

CLAIRE: I thought you'd be the best one to tell. You're supposedly a man of God.

CALVIN: More like a man *from* God. I'm just a messenger.

CLAIRE: You don't believe in life after death?

CALVIN: This sounds more like *death* after death. Nothing happens.

CLAIRE: Look. I think I would have found out a little more if I hadn't been pulled back here.

CALVIN: Were you pulled? Or were you *pushed*?

CLAIRE: Oh, fuck off.

CALVIN: Why is that not a relevant question? That might be important.

CLAIRE: For God's sake.

CALVIN: Good idea, let's talk about Him for a minute. You're telling me this is part of God's plan?

CLAIRE: No. I'm not.

CALVIN: Good. So as I'm sure you realize, this had to be a dream—

CLAIRE: No. Not a dream—

CALVIN: All right, sorry to use such a pedestrian word, let's say hallucination—

CLAIRE: Damn it, Calvin—

CALVIN: Whatever you want to call it—did you see God?

CLAIRE: No. But to tell you the truth…

CALVIN: What? Go on. Did you hear Him? Did He speak to you?

CLAIRE: No. Nobody spoke to me. But I had the impression—scratch that, the total certainty…

CALVIN: That God was watching you?

CLAIRE: Just the opposite. That no one was watching me. God wasn't there.

CALVIN: What do you mean?

CLAIRE: He wasn't there.

CALVIN: What do you mean he wasn't there? You mean he wasn't sitting on a heavenly throne with a golden clipboard and a hand stamp? I would hope you wouldn't expect such a thing.

CLAIRE: No. I mean that…wherever I was, whatever I was doing there…

CALVIN: Grazing in the grass—

CLAIRE: I knew for a fact—God had never been there. He didn't have anything to do with it. He didn't exist.

CALVIN: You mean…at all?

CLAIRE: I mean at all.

CALVIN: What good is an afterlife for if you don't get to meet God? That's a pretty big letdown.

CLAIRE: It felt like…no other way to say this…like *I* was God.

(*Pause.* CALVIN *stands up and turns away.*)

CALVIN: Okay, I'm done here.

CLAIRE: Don't go.

(CALVIN *turns back with anger.*)

CALVIN: Claire, you said you wanted me to listen. I've listened. You said you wanted my feedback as a brother and as a minister. As a brother, you're clearly still suffering the afteraffects of a traumatic brain injury, and you're mixing up reality with some bizarre, half-comatose fantasy. That's me giving you the benefit of the doubt, as your brother. But as a minister, I think you should know that everything you just said is highly offensive to what I believe and the teachings to which I've devoted my life. You're trying to convince me that our ultimate destiny is the most unglorious, inhuman and generally pointless depiction of eternity I've ever heard. I would even prefer Gus's vision of total nothingness. I don't agree with that, but at least that idea is worthy of debate. You're talking about a field of grass. No enlightenment, no purpose, no redemption, no salvation. Just grass. I deserve some salvation, you understand? We deserve something for our troubles. We deserve to get a hall pass from God and enter his Kingdom. To you, for some reason, it feels nice for you to think of death as a mediocre landscape painting, but it does nothing for me.

CLAIRE: Maybe it's not for you, Calvin. Or anyone else. Maybe it was only for me. It was my reward. And I was happy when I was there.

CALVIN: Only for you. So life after death is made to order? Like ordering a personal pizza?

CLAIRE: Why not?

CALVIN: Because every single book and chapter of the scriptures talks about how we'll come together when we die. We don't go our separate ways. Heaven isn't for hermits.

CLAIRE: I keep telling you, it didn't seem like Heaven.

CALVIN: The first thing you've said that I agree with.

CLAIRE: Well, at least there's that.

CALVIN: Now, back to the real world. I will get your purse, grab your house keys, and come back with some unexciting clothes for you to wear so you can leave here. Then I'll take you home where you can go to sleep in the usual way, and have some normal dreams involving food or flying or fucking like other people do. And Rosie will be there to shake you back into reality before you have the chance to return to your Little Lack of a House on the Prairie.

CLAIRE: All right, all right.

CALVIN: Only promise me this. You will not cause your stepsister or your stepfather any undue concern by repeating this insanity to them. I don't want them worrying about your mental state. So don't mention any of this to them. Okay?

CLAIRE: Okay, okay.

CALVIN: Promise?

CLAIRE: Promise.

(CALVIN *holds out his little finger.*)

CALVIN: Pinky swear?

CLAIRE: Don't be childish.

CALVIN: I've never been more adult in my life. Pinky swear!

(*Pause.* CLAIRE *wraps her little finger around* CALVIN's.)

CLAIRE: Pinky swear. I won't say a word.

Scene Three

(GUS' study)

(Monday night)

(GUS is in his chair near the fireplace, while CALVIN stokes the fire and ROSIE serves coffee.)

GUS: Grass? Nothing but grass?

ROSIE: That's what she told me.

CALVIN: I asked Claire not to say anything. I begged her.

ROSIE: She said that too.

CALVIN: Did she mention that she swore an oath?

ROSIE: A pinky swear? I don't think that counts.

GUS: This doesn't sound like her. She was always so level headed.

CALVIN: She still is. These are just the aftereffects of her injury.

ROSIE: I don't think so.

GUS: Did she seem woozy to you? Out of it?

ROSIE: I stayed with her all day yesterday. She seemed fine.

CALVIN: It's too soon to know. She shouldn't have gone back to school today.

GUS: Anything happen there?

ROSIE: No. Well, maybe.

GUS: What?

ROSIE: Her Comparative Religion was a little weird.

CALVIN: How so?

ROSIE: She threw out today's lesson. And switched to talking about how different religions see life after death.

CALVIN: Uh-oh.

ROSIE: She talked about the Egyptians, and the Greeks and Romans, and Islam, and heaven, and hell, and purgatory, and reincarnation. She was talking really fast.

CALVIN: I better call her. (*He pulls out his phone.*)

ROSIE: She kind of slowed down when she talked about Hinduism.

CALVIN: Of course she did. They believe in being reborn when you die. She probably thinks that she— (*To his phone*) Claire? Why aren't you in bed like they told you? …Of course I'm pissed. A pinky swear used to mean something to you… Wait, are you driving? …Because it's dark out, and still icy, and you had a concussion, remember? Where are you going that's so important? (*He sighs, and tells the others.*) She's bringing ribs. (*Back to her*) We don't need them.

GUS: Speak for yourself!

CALVIN: Don't listen to Gus. Get off the phone and go home now…right…okay. (*He puts his phone away.*) She'll be here soon. No doubt to continue today's lecture on reincarnation.

ROSIE: I don't think I believe in that.

CALVIN: Nor should you, Rosie. Christians believe in the Soul.

GUS: Bah. It's all the same nonsense. Crutches for people who are afraid to die.

ROSIE: Aren't you afraid to die, Dad?

GUS: I'm not looking forward to it. But I'm prepared for it.

CALVIN: How does an atheist even do that?

GUS: I know that my time on earth is limited. And I've got to spend every minute of every day as though it were my last.

CALVIN: By reading Facebook and watching Antique Roadshow?

GUS: See, this is where you religious types show limited thinking. I'm not talking about how I spend my days. I'm talking about mental preparation.

ROSIE: For what?

GUS: For nothing. Because that's what happens after we die—nothing.

ROSIE: That can't be right.

CALVIN: It's not.

GUS: It is. You really think our time on this earth is just about what happens after? All about reward and punishment, like winning a free trip to Italy on The Price is Right? That's how most human beings live. Well, it's not for me. I have more pride than that.

CALVIN: Or stubbornness.

GUS: Call it whatever you like. I just refuse to live my life according to fairy tales. When we die, that's it. No peace, no salvation, no coming back as a princess or a cockroach. No memories. No you. No me. No anything. That's it. The end. Nada.

ROSIE: That is so depressing.

CALVIN: Young minds, Gus.

ROSIE: Life has no meaning without God.

GUS: See, I find *that* depressing. That you would say that.

CALVIN: Gus—

GUS: No, Rosie's sixteen. She can hear this without freaking out. God doesn't give our lives meaning. We do. We are the gods and goddesses of our own existence.

CALVIN: I'm not a god. And neither are you.

GUS: I can't speak for you. But I am responsible for my own decisions. My own fate.

CALVIN: That's not the same as divinity.

GUS: I never said it was. I'm just saying God is irrelevant to our daily lives.

ROSIE: Oh wow.

CALVIN: This isn't a big deal, Rosie. It's called humanism.

GUS: It's called common sense. I don't need the prospect of some future existence to be a better human being.

ROSIE: Some people do.

GUS: Sure they do. That's the problem.

ROSIE: What do you have against Christians, anyway?

CALVIN: Oh, that's the ten million dollar question.

GUS: I was baptized a Catholic, you know. Stayed one until I was your age.

ROSIE: What changed your mind?

GUS: A book report. Let me see if I can find the book. I'll show it to you. *(With some effort, he gets up and looks for a book on the shelf.)*

CALVIN: Never mind, Gus.

GUS: Wait a minute…found it.

(GUS pulls out the book and hands it to ROSIE.)

GUS: Ever hear of it?

(ROSIE *examines the book.*)

ROSIE: James Joyce.

GUS: That's right.

ROSIE: I've heard of him. But I've never read anything by him.

CALVIN: No one does any more. Outside of English majors.

ROSIE: *(Reading the title) Portrait of the Artist as a Young Man.*

GUS: That's how they tried to indoctrinate us in Catholic school. By making us read that.

ROSIE: What's wrong with it?

GUS: About halfway through, there's a very long passage where an Irish priest describes the torments of Hell. It's all very literal, fire and brimstone, physical torture, despair and agony.

CALVIN: I think Joyce meant to be satiric.

GUS: Well, I didn't think it was funny. I threw the book right across my room without reading another word. I didn't do the book report, got an F, and decided right there and then that religion was all stuff and nonsense.

ROSIE: Why did they make you read it, if it's so awful?

GUS: Excellent question. Because, my darling daughter, all religion is designed to achieve one thing, and one thing only. *Fear.*

CALVIN: Now *that's* nonsense.

GUS: Look, I may not have your advanced degree in theology, but I'm not uneducated. My business degree is right up there on the wall if you want to look at it.

CALVIN: I'm not calling you stupid.

Gus: Glad to hear it. So if you'll stop interrupting me, I'll let you put me down *after* I'm finished.

Calvin: Go ahead.

(Gus *turns back to* Rosie.)

Gus: As I was saying. That's how religions control the masses. Fear. Fear of death. Because from the beginning of time, mankind hasn't been too thrilled about the fact that everybody dies. We don't always know when, and we certainly never know why. So it brings most people comfort to think there's something waiting for us after we're all done here. And they usually like to imagine it might be nicer. Now, here's the catch. Some folks don't like the idea of mingling with other types of people. They created segregation and discrimination here, so they decided to transfer the same idea to the afterlife. They created Heaven and Hell, the Good Place and the Bad Place, whatever names you wanna give them. And the angels make you stand in two lines, like you're back in school and being picked for dodgeball.

Calvin: Not the same thing.

Gus: Pretty close. *(To* Rosie*)* Now does that make sense to you?

Rosie: You left something out.

Gus: Like what?

Rosie: Like Jesus Christ.

Calvin: Hear, hear.

Gus: Look, I give Jesus plenty of credit. He was like the best timeshare salesman who ever lived. Telling everybody about the waterfront property with excellent weather and fishing. Then when you get there it's nothing but sand.

Calvin: Or grass.

GUS: Apparently.

ROSIE: I kind of liked what Claire said about it.

CALVIN: You did?

ROSIE: Yeah.

CALVIN: Even the godless part?

ROSIE: She wasn't there long enough to see God. That was just the first place she saw. And she liked it. Maybe it was just for her, like she said. It doesn't mean that's all there is. I told her that.

CALVIN: Did she agree?

ROSIE: No. She thinks that was it.

CALVIN: And that disturbs you, doesn't it?

ROSIE: Well, yeah. It would disturb anybody.

GUS: Not me. Because I know there isn't anything after we die.

ROSIE: That's even more disturbing.

CALVIN: I'm with Rosie.

GUS: Because you're both too afraid to accept the simple truth.

CALVIN: You don't know what's true, Gus. Nobody knows. That's why faith is so important.

GUS: It's a crutch.

ROSIE: Hey. Did you forget about my plan?

GUS: I'm sorry, Rosie. I don't want to hurt your feelings. I know you think there's something beautiful about being a nun, but that's just another fantasy. Religion is just one big distraction.

ROSIE: So you don't believe in anything.

(GUS *goes to the desk and picks up a laminated chart.*)

GUS: Not so. I believe in this. That's based on scientific research.

(GUS *hands it to* ROSIE.)

ROSIE: This is just a bunch of numbers.

GUS: That's right. Those are called actuarial tables.

CALVIN: Oh for God's sake.

GUS: Which gets updated every year so it stays current. It predicts the average life expectancy of people. Those are the factors that affect life insurance rates.

ROSIE: Life insurance.

GUS: There are variables, of course. My own life expectancy is probably shorter than that indicates, since I'm recovering from prostate cancer. So I probably won't live as long as you will.

ROSIE: I don't want to hear about this stuff.

CALVIN: You're stressing her out, Gus.

GUS: All right, enough about us. Let's go back to my point.

ROSIE: Which is what?

GUS: Which is this—religion is also selling insurance. Not life insurance. Death insurance.

CALVIN: That's a terrible thing to say.

GUS: Absolutely. Insurance about what happens after you die. Almost all religions claim that if you walk the straight and narrow, they can insure that you'll see the gates of heaven. They just have different versions.

CALVIN: This is really reductive.

GUS: It's like Santa Claus. He sees what you are doing, he knows if you've been good. Santa Claus is God for kids who are too young to understand religion. Electric train or a lump of coal. Heaven or Hell. It's that simple.

CALVIN: So much for four years of divinity school.

ROSIE: I don't think you're right about any of this.

GUS: You're still young, honey. Just think about what I've said and I know you'll come around. Just like your mother did.

CALVIN: She did no such thing. She was a practicing Presbyterian.

GUS: Sure, she went through the motions. For your sake.

CALVIN: My sake?

GUS: She only went to your services because you needed better attendance during Covid. That's what killed her.

(Pause)

CALVIN: Finally. You've been hinting around at this for a year. Now it comes out.

GUS: Never mind.

CALVIN: You blame me for Mom's death.

GUS: Not you specifically. Your stupid Sunday services. She had to watch her precious son all dressed up and performing for the old folks who are scared to die. No matter how dangerous.

CALVIN: All right. I've been biting my tongue too long. Now you're gonna listen to me.

(GUS *gets to his feet.)*

GUS: Feel free. I won't stop you.

(ROSIE *finds her cell phone and dials.)*

CALVIN: We're going to have it out once and for all.

ROSIE: *(On her phone)* Claire? Things are getting weird over here. Listen. *(She holds her phone out.)*

GUS: Where else could she get it?

CALVIN: Anywhere. The grocery. Going on neighborhood walks. Maybe from you.

GUS: Me? I never had it.

CALVIN: You don't know that.

ROSIE: Can you guys stop this?

CALVIN: I actually encouraged her to stay home from church. I told her it was safer and God would understand. But she wouldn't hear of it. She came because of you..

GUS: Me? How do you figure that?

CALVIN: She came to pray for you.

(*Pause*)

GUS: No way. I told her the futility of prayer. She gave it up.

CALVIN: That's just what she told you, Gus. She loved you and didn't want you to get upset while you were in remission.

GUS: Bullshit.

ROSIE: He's right, Dad.

(GUS *turns to* ROSIE.)

GUS: You know something about this?

ROSIE: I once saw her praying while you were taking a shower. She told me not to tell you.

GUS: What do you mean by praying?

ROSIE: I mean she was on her knees by the side of the bed. Talking to God.

GUS: So she hid that from me?

CALVIN: All the time.

ROSIE: She told me not to tell you. That her prayers kept you from dying. And that Jesus would keep you alive as long as she did them.

GUS: I don't believe that. You're making this up.

ROSIE: Why would I?

CALVIN: It's true, Gus. Mom talked to me about too. In private.

GUS: So it was a conspiracy. Between all of you. Claire too, I suppose.

CALVIN: Yes. She knew.

GUS: I never needed anyone's prayers.

CALVIN: She thought you did.

GUS: Why? Because I was sick?

CALVIN: Not just that. Because you were damned.

(We hear a door slam.)

ROSIE: Okay, Claire's here now. Please stop this. She's still recoverin—

(CLAIRE comes in, wearing her coat, carrying a takeout bag and holding the phone to her ear.)

CLAIRE: This is stupid, guys. Stop it now.

CALVIN: He's getting upset for no reason.

GUS: No reason? He just called me damned. *(Turning to* CALVIN*)* How dare you talk to me that way? Who do you think you are?

CALVIN: I don't think anything. That isn't my word. It was hers. She thought you were heading for eternal damnation. She said so.

CLAIRE: What if she did? It's just a word. It doesn't mean anything.

GUS: You heard her say it too?

CLAIRE: It worried her, Gus. She loved you. And she got tired of you taking this atheistic…pose.

GUS: *Pose*? She thought it was a pose? My whole fucking belief system is a pose?

CLAIRE: Aren't they all? I think we can all agree on that by now.

CALVIN: Well I don't!

ROSIE: Claire! You're not helping!

GUS: You're all a bunch of fucking liars!

CALVIN: Why would we lie?

GUS: You most of all. You talked her into this—this childish bullshit about heaven and hell.

CALVIN: Me? I don't even believe in Hell.

GUS: The hell you don't.

CALVIN: It's not a big thing with Presbyterians. At least not as an actual place. John Calvin thought Hell represented man's separation from God. I think Mom was worried about that with you.

GUS: To the point where she had to go to your stupid fucking church to pray for my soul. You did kill her.

ROSIE: Stop it, Dad!

CLAIRE: Okay, Gus. You're being ridiculous.

GUS: Because you knew I was winning!

CALVIN: *Winning*? What the—

GUS: And you couldn't bear it. You and your precious God. You had to drag her back into this nonsense. Until you *killed* her!

ROSIE: Dad!

CALVIN: You have no fucking right to say that. I told her to stay home. You know that. Of all the people who *didn't* need to attend church during a pandemic—

GUS: You were jealous!

CALVIN: Of *what*?

CLAIRE: Gus, shut up. Why are you getting so worked up? Our mom loved you and prayed for you. Why is that so awful?

GUS: Because if she prayed, it was to a God who TOOK HER AWAY FROM ME!

ROSIE: NOT JUST YOU!

(*Pause.* CLAIRE *goes to* ROSIE *and puts her arm around her.*)

CLAIRE: That's right, Rosie. All of us.

(*Long pause.* GUS *slowly sits. The others try to calm down, turning inward.*)

GUS: So there you have it. Does God make sense to any of you? Where's our reward? We're basically good people. He's supposed to reward the good. Isn't he? Why did he take his eye off the ball? Why would He do this to us? (*Turning to* CALVIN) You're supposed to have all the answers. Tell us why.

CLAIRE: Leave him alone, Gus.

CALVIN: No. He's right. This is my job. Everyone turn to me and I'll explain it all. It all makes sense if you just hear the reasons. And I can tell you the reasons. That's my job. It's a test of faith. It's all part of God's plan. I'm here to explain it.

CLAIRE: Just stop, Calvin.

CALVIN: Stop? How can I stop? It never does stop. Over and over and over. Each and every day. That's why I'm here. It's my duty to provide answers and comfort. But I can't. Not any more.

CLAIRE: It doesn't matter.

CALVIN: Exactly. Those are the truest words we've heard here tonight.

ROSIE: But you're a minister.

CALVIN: I'm not a minister. I'm a border collie. I keep trying to circle around the sheep, and keep them in line, but they're bored with my pompous piety. I don't blame them. I bore myself.

ROSIE: You don't mean any of this.

CALVIN: Who knows what I mean? I'm a fraud. Trying to convince people to believe in things I don't believe myself.

ROSIE: But you have to believe!

CALVIN: Sorry to let you down, Rosie. I know I'm a disappointment.

CLAIRE: You're not.

CALVIN: Gus is right, you know.

GUS: You don't have to say that.

CALVIN: Don't back down now, Gus. Everyone *is* afraid. We all are. Everything we do to try and crowbar some meaning into our lives—is because we're terrified.

ROSIE: Of what?

CALVIN: Nobody knows. There's no answer in anything we try. We just pretend. That's not what faith is supposed to be. But that's what it is. We just pretend to believe in God. We're all a bunch of heathens, worshipping anything that makes us less afraid. (*He reaches for the Bible next to Carolyn's picture.*) Including this, I guess. The word of God? Or a book of fiction? It's impossible to say, even after two thousand years. And not nearly as big a seller as *Fifty Shades of Gray.*

ROSIE: Isn't that a dirty book? That's a terrible comparison.

CALVIN: Yes, it is. One might even call it blasphemy. But for blasphemy to work, you have to blaspheme something that people believe in. Nobody believes this claptrap any more. Why bother keeping it around?

GUS: Put that down! It belonged to Carolyn.

CALVIN: You of all people shouldn't care what happens to this stupid, pointless book! (*He's about to fling the Bible into the fireplace, pulling his arm back.*)

CLAIRE:	ROSIE:	GUS:
CALVIN!	STOP IT!	NO!

(GUS *lurches out of his chair, but falls, obviously riddled with pain.*)

(CALVIN *sees him and stops what he's doing. The others rush to his aid.*)

CALVIN: Gus?

ROSIE: Daddy? What's wrong?

CLAIRE: Oh my God.

GUS: Give…it…to me.

(CALVIN *kneels down next to him and hands him the Bible.*)

GUS: It was…hers.

Scene Four

(*Another hospital room*)

(*Wednesday morning*)

(*Same set up as before, with the hospital bed, the partition, and the folding chair.*)

(*Except this time it is* GUS *who lies in the bed, hooked up to the IV tower. He is reading the same book he showed* ROSIE *earlier, his face obscured as he holds it up to his eyes.*)

(CLAIRE *tiptoes in, in case he's asleep. She sees him reading.*)

CLAIRE: Gus?

GUS: Not now.

CLAIRE: It's Claire.

(GUS *lowers the book and looks at her. His eyes are wet.*)

GUS: Oh. Sorry. I thought you were the nurse.

CLAIRE: Are you crying?

(GUS *self-consciously wipes his tears.*)

GUS: Of course not. It's very humid in here.

CLAIRE: You don't have to do that with me. What's wrong?

GUS: Okay. Nothing's wrong. It's just…

(GUS *holds the book out, and* CLAIRE *takes it.*)

CLAIRE: James Joyce?

GUS: That is a fucking brilliant book.

CLAIRE: I thought you hated it.

GUS: I did hate it. I was just reminding myself how much I hated it.

CLAIRE: Here's an idea. Don't read it.

GUS: No, I was wrong to hate that thing my whole life. After you get through the Hell part, it all comes together. He rejects everything he was taught, just like I did. And he figures out who he wants to be.

CLAIRE: So now you relate to it.

GUS: Sure. He became a writer. I became a claims adjuster. That's the only difference.

CLAIRE: Practically identical.

GUS: I'm only about ten pages from the end.

CLAIRE: Maybe I shouldn't have interrupted you.

GUS: Not at all. I've got plenty of time to finish it. Plenty of time.

CLAIRE: Any word on when they'll be releasing you?

GUS: No. They still want to do some tests. I guess I'll let them. But I expect I'll be out by tomorrow. The day after at the latest. *(He suddenly grimaces.)*

CLAIRE: Gus? What is it?

(GUS slowly relaxes again.)

GUS: Nothing. Just my stitches.

CLAIRE: How does it feel to be without a prostate?

GUS: Glad to be rid of it. But I can't even get hold of a pain pill without calling that damn nurse.

CLAIRE: Should I call her for you?

GUS: I wouldn't give her the satisfaction. I can hold out.

CLAIRE: That's silly. If you're in pain—

GUS: It comes and goes. Don't worry about it. I'm fine now. How is everybody? I don't want anybody worrying about me.

CLAIRE: We're not.

GUS: Who's here now?

CLAIRE: Everyone. But they won't let us all come in at once. Only one at a time.

GUS: More bullshit. But I guess I can see that. I'm not at my best.

CLAIRE: You will be soon.

GUS: Oh sure, sure. You say Calvin's here too?

CLAIRE: Yes. Right outside. He's mortified. He thinks he caused this.

GUS: Did you tell him otherwise?

CLAIRE: Yes. But I don't think he believes me. He wants to hear it from you.

GUS: Good. I'll let him stew a little bit. Serves him right.

CLAIRE: You need to see him. Make it right between you.

GUS: Oh, I will. I promise you. I actually have something important to ask him.

CLAIRE: Like what?

GUS: A favor. You can tell him that. How's teaching?

CLAIRE: I'm not sure. My classes felt a bit rote today. I feel a little lost.

GUS: Because of what you saw the last night you were here.

CLAIRE: Yeah. Or what I might have seen.

GUS: Uh-oh. You're having second thoughts?

CLAIRE: Well, the longer I'm away from it, the more I wonder.

GUS: So now you're not sure what to believe.

CLAIRE: I guess so.

GUS: You feel a little less special, I guess. Your faith is shaken.

CLAIRE: You could say that. How about you? Still certain there's nothing beyond this world?

GUS: More sure than ever. I have great faith in my faithlessness.

CLAIRE: I think you just like being perverse.

GUS: There's probably a little of that too. *(He suddenly grimaces again.)*

CLAIRE: Gus?

GUS: Just…a minute. (*He breathes out and relaxes.*)

CLAIRE: I'm getting the nurse.

GUS: No. Not yet. Come here. This is important.

(GUS *motions for* CLAIRE *to come closer.*)

GUS: I'm going to be fine. I promise you.

CLAIRE: I know that.

GUS: On the other hand, no one can predict everything. So just in case—

(CLAIRE *backs away quickly.*)

CLAIRE: Stop it, Dad! I don't want to hear it.

GUS: It's okay. Sit down.

(CLAIRE *does so, and calms herself.*)

GUS: Do you realize you just called me Dad?

CLAIRE: I did?

GUS: For the first time.

CLAIRE: I'm sorry. I'm very upset.

GUS: Don't apologize. I liked it.

CLAIRE: A little late, I suppose.

GUS: Better late than never. Which brings me back to what I need to tell you. Again, chances are you won't have to know this, but I want you to listen anyway.

CLAIRE: Just in case.

GUS: Exactly. Everything you all will need is in my top desk drawer in the library. It appoints you as the executor.

CLAIRE: Why me?

GUS: Because I say so. It's a simple will. Everything gets divided evenly between you, Calvin and Rosie. With one exception. Rosie gets the house.

CLAIRE: I can see that.

GUS: I figured you would. That's all. We're done talking about that.

CLAIRE: Thank God. I can't take anymore.

GUS: One more thing.

CLAIRE: You just said—

GUS: Shut up and listen. I don't want any kind of service. No talk of God or redemption. Especially from Calvin. Just stare at me in the box, then shove the box into the oven. You can play rock, paper, scissors to see who pushes the button.

CLAIRE: Stop it.

GUS: You can put the jar wherever you like. As a doorstop if you want.

CLAIRE: This is incredibly morbid.

GUS: All right. Put the jar next to your mother's picture. It can replace the Bible.

(CLAIRE *begins to tear up, angry.*)

CLAIRE: Fuck you, Gus. You're going right into the columbarium next to mom's ashes. Whether you like it or not. Because I don't care about your wishes. She would want you there. Got it?

(*Pause.* GUS *is surprised.*)

(*He begins to protest, but stops himself. He smiles.*)

GUS: Sounds good. Thank you.

CLAIRE: You're welcome.

GUS: All right, sweetheart. You can send in the next victim.

CLAIRE: Calvin?

GUS: I'll save him for last. He can squirm.

CLAIRE: You really are a cruel bastard, aren't you?

GUS: Just having a little fun. Tell Rosie to come in now.

(CLAIRE *wipes her eyes.*)

CLAIRE: Okay. Bye. Dad.

GUS: See you tomorrow.

(CLAIRE *exits.*)

(*Pause.* GUS *composes himself, tries to adjust his bed so he can sit up.*)

(ROSIE *enters.* GUS *smiles broadly at her.*)

GUS: There's my girl.

(ROSIE *makes a beeline for her to hug him.*)

GUS: Careful, careful, not too hard. Your old man is a bit fragile.

ROSIE: What's wrong? Are you in pain?

GUS: Of course not. Just a little tired. They come in every twenty minutes to jab my arm or stuff a pill down my throat. Hard to get any rest.

ROSIE: I won't stay long.

GUS: No hurry. Tell me how you are. What's new?

ROSIE: Since yesterday?

GUS: Sure. A lot can happen in a day. Look at me.

ROSIE: Yeah.

GUS: How was school?

ROSIE: I don't know. Hard to concentrate, knowing you were here.

GUS: You didn't miss anything, believe me. There's nothing you could have done. Especially after they decided I wasn't in immediate danger.

ROSIE: They called it a relapse.

GUS: That doesn't mean anything. I'll be out of here in a day or two. That's what I told Claire.

ROSIE: I've been in the chapel. Praying. Hope you don't mind.

GUS: Not at all. I appreciate the good words.

ROSIE: Even though you don't think anyone listens.

GUS: I appreciate *your* words, Rosie. It doesn't matter who hears you. *(Short pause)* Can I ask you something? In all honesty?

ROSIE: Yes.

GUS: Did you think your mom and I…are you glad that we adopted you?

ROSIE: Of course!

GUS: Did you think we were good parents? Did we treat you right?

ROSIE: Dad, this is embarassing.

GUS: Because what Claire and Calvin said, that you might want to become a nun because you missed the orphanage—any truth in that?

ROSIE: No way. I feel so lucky that you found me. Don't you know that?

GUS: I thought I did, but I've been having some doubts.

ROSIE: I don't miss that place at all. Or the nuns either. I just miss Mom.

(GUS takes ROSIE's hand.)

GUS: Me too, baby. Me too. So we gave you enough love? That's all I want to know.

ROSIE: More than enough, Dad.

GUS: I shouldn't have gotten so mad.

ROSIE: You didn't do anything wrong. In my opinion.

GUS: Well, that's the opinion of a future nun. So that counts a lot.

ROSIE: Calvin doesn't think so either. He was just mad about other stuff. And himself.

GUS: Is that what he told you?

ROSIE: That's what I told him. He agreed.

GUS: You're a very bright girl, Rosie. I'm very proud of you. No matter what you decide to do with your life.

ROSIE: Really?

GUS: Absolutely. It's your life to live. You don't have to answer to me or anyone else. You're practically a woman. You'll know what to do.

ROSIE: Thank you daddy.

(ROSIE *hugs* GUS *again. He grimaces.*)

GUS: Gently, gently.

(ROSIE *lets go.*)

ROSIE: Can I send Calvin in now? He's so anxious to see you.

GUS: Go ahead. Tell him I'm ready.

ROSIE: You won't yell at him, will you? Cause I know he won't yell at you.

GUS: I promise. Tell him I want him to read something to me.

ROSIE: What?

GUS: The end of a book. Before they turn down the lights. He loves to read things out loud. He'll enjoy it.

ROSIE: I'll tell him.

GUS: See you tomorrow.

ROSIE: Okay. Bye.

(GUS *watches her go, sadly.*)

(He picks up the book, and finds the place where he left his bookmark.)

Scene Five

(GUS's study)

(One week later)

(ROSIE and CALVIN are there. There is a bottle of wine and some glasses on the desk.)

(ROSIE is picking up GUS' old sweater from his usual chair. She smells it and puts it on. CALVIN is crouched down by the fire.)

(CLAIRE enters the room, carrying a box with flowers, pictures, etc. She is dressed in black, and her bandage is finally gone.)

CLAIRE: Gus would have really hated this day.

CALVIN: Obviously.

CLAIRE: I mean—

CALVIN: I know what you mean.

(When CALVIN rises and turns, we notice that he is dressed—for the first time—as a Presbyterian minister, in a clerical collar.)

CLAIRE: I half expected him to jump up from the coffin when you walked in dressed like that.

ROSIE: It was a beautiful service.

CLAIRE: Yes, it was, Calvin. Thank you for taking it over.

ROSIE: But you're right. Dad would have hated it.

CALVIN: I didn't do it for him. I did it us. And for the others. The living need special comfort on days like this. The friends and family he left behind.

ROSIE: There sure were a lot of them.

CLAIRE: Yeah. So many people I didn't know.

CALVIN: He had a big impact.

CLAIRE: You did a great job.

CALVIN: It helped that I knew him a little.

CLAIRE: And you didn't hide his atheism.

CALVIN: No, that wouldn't have been right.

ROSIE: What was that joke you told? I'm not sure I got it.

CALVIN: It was from Gus. He loved to collect atheist jokes.

ROSIE: Do it again.

(CALVIN *demurs.*)

ROSIE: Come on.

CALVIN: All right. An atheist is fishing out in the middle of the Loch Ness. Suddenly, Nessie comes up under him, throwing him and his boat up into the air.

ROSIE: What's a Nessie?

CALVIN: The Loch Ness monster. There's a myth of a monster, about a thousand years old, in this lake in Scotland. Like a giant sea serpent or a brontosaurus.

ROSIE: Oh. I never heard of it.

CLAIRE: We should have a class in cryptozoology at school.

CALVIN: So anyway, the ferocious beast tosses the atheist way up into the air, and opens its massive jaws wide to prepare to eat him. While in the air, the man cries out, "Oh God, help me!" Suddenly all time stops, and the man freezes in mid-air. God appears next to him and says, "Oh really? All your life you've denied that I exist, and now you expect me to save you?" And the man replies, "Oh, give me a frickin' break! I didn't believe in this thing either, until a minute ago!"

(ROSIE *looks confused.*)

CALVIN: You don't think it's funny?

ROSIE: Is that it?

CALVIN: What more do you want?

ROSIE: Did he get eaten or not?

CALVIN: That's not the point. Never mind.

ROSIE: Maybe when Dad told it, it was funnier.

CALVIN: I'm sure it was.

CLAIRE: You know what would have really pissed Gus off today? That Catholic priest who showed up out of nowhere. Who invited him? Nobody knew him at all.

CALVIN: Gus did.

CLAIRE: How do you know?

CALVIN: That priest heard his confession. And gave him last rites.

(*Pause*)

CLAIRE: That's impossible.

CALVIN: It's true.

CLAIRE: What? Who arranged for that?

CALVIN: I did. He asked me to.

ROSIE: Dad wanted a Catholic priest? Before he died?

CLAIRE: I don't believe it.

CALVIN: I found it hard to believe myself. That last night he asked me to read James Joyce to him. I finished the last sentence, looked up and he was crying.

CLAIRE: Me too! I found him crying over that same damn book.

ROSIE: Why? How does it end?

CALVIN: "Old father, old artificer, stand me now and ever in good stead."

ROSIE: What does that mean?

CALVIN: Who knows? It's Joyce.

CLAIRE: Calvin—

CALVIN: The young man's name is Stephen Daedalus. A reference to Greek myth.

ROSIE: I remember Daedalus. He built wings out of wax for his son Icarus. So they could fly out of the labyrinth.

CLAIRE: All right! One point for private school education.

CALVIN: But I don't think Gus understood the reference to "father". He asked me to arrange for a priest. And not to tell either of you.

CLAIRE: And you encouraged him, didn't you?

CALVIN: Just the opposite. I told him this contradicted a lifetime of atheism. It must be his medicine making him talk that way. He wasn't himself.

CLAIRE: Good for you.

CALVIN: But he insisted he wanted a priest. He grabbed my hand, stared right into my eyes, and said, "What if I'm wrong?"

(Pause)

CLAIRE: Wow. So even Gus had a crisis of faith at the end. *(She takes a picture of* GUS *out of the box and puts it on the mantle.)*

ROSIE: Or…he finally *found* it.

CALVIN: Either way, he managed to sell himself one last insurance policy. *(He grabs a wine glass and holds it up to the picture.)* To Gus.

(CLAIRE *and* ROSIE *hold up their glass and bottle.*)

CLAIRE: To Gus.

ROSIE: To Dad.

(CLAIRE *points to a photo album propped up on the mantle.*)

CLAIRE: What's this thing? A scrapbook?

CALVIN: Oh! I almost forgot. (*He puts down his glass and picks up the album.*) It's an old photo album.

ROSIE: One of Dad's?

CALVIN: No. It's mine. I was looking for old pictures of Gus that we could use today. And I found this. From when Claire and I were kids.

CLAIRE: No kidding! Let me see it.

CALVIN: Exactly why I brought it. Go to about five pages in.

(CALVIN *hands the album to* CLAIRE, *who eagerly looks inside. Her expression changes, stunned by what she sees.*)

CLAIRE: What is this?

CALVIN: Look familiar?

CLAIRE: How could this be in here?

CALVIN: Because you were there. Like you said. You were actually there.

ROSIE: Where? (*She goes over to look over* CLAIRE'S *shoulder.*)

CLAIRE: This is the place I saw. The night I almost died.

ROSIE: That's a lot of grass.

CALVIN: You saw it then because you'd seen it before. You were remembering something from your childhood.

(CLAIRE *looks up at* CALVIN.)

CLAIRE: What is it?

CALVIN: Remember the road trip we took to the southwest? The one where we saw the Grand Canyon?

CLAIRE: Not very well. I was pretty young.

CALVIN: Mom and Dad stopped there on the way back. It's near the border of Kansas and Oklahoma.

CLAIRE: It was called something. It had a name.

CALVIN: Tallgrass Prairie Preserve.

CLAIRE: Oh my God.

CALVIN: When I saw that picture, I remembered it. We were there all right. It was Mom's idea to stop the car there. The two of you got out and explored. Dad stayed in the car and took a nap. I stayed with him and read comic books.

CLAIRE: Mom. Mom was with me.

CALVIN: That was the most boring place on the most boring drive I've ever been forced to take. There was nothing there. Nothing at all.

ROSIE: It looks beautiful.

CLAIRE: And look! In the distance. Big black shapes. What are they?

(A teasing pause)

CALVIN: Bison.

CLAIRE: Yes! Of course.

CALVIN: One of the last surviving herds, apparently.

ROSIE: Wow. It's like going back in time.

CALVIN: Which is exactly what Claire did.

ROSIE: Does this make you change your mind, Claire? Do you still think there's life after death?

CLAIRE: Yes. I do.

CALVIN: And it involves grass?

CLAIRE: For me it does. I was alone with my mother. And we had never been closer than we were alone together on that prairie. That might have been the happiest day of my life.

CALVIN: Kind of a low bar, don't you think?

CLAIRE: Probably. But it makes sense to me that I ended up back there.

ROSIE: Maybe if you'd stayed longer, you would have seen Mom.

CLAIRE: Maybe so. (*She turns to* CALVIN.) Thanks for solving the mystery, Calvin.

CALVIN: Kind of a let down, I guess.

CLAIRE: Not to me. I'm thrilled. (*She puts down the photo album.*) Next item on the agenda. (*She opens the desk drawer and pulls out a large manila envelope.*) Here it is. Just as he said it would be.

CALVIN: He told me you'd be the executor.

CLAIRE: You don't mind?

CALVIN: I prefer it.

CLAIRE: I'll go over this with a lawyer. But one thing we already discussed. And that's Rosie's situation.

ROSIE: I have a situation?

CLAIRE: You do indeed. Your dad left you this house. To own and live in.

(ROSIE *is stunned. She looks around.*)

ROSIE: Oh wow. You guys aren't mad?

CALVIN: Not at all. It's the way it should be.

ROSIE: So I'm gonna live here by myself?

CLAIRE: I don't think that's possible, Rosie. Not till you're older. So one of us will move in here with you. The question is—which one of us? Me or—

ROSIE: *(To* CLAIRE, *quickly)* You.

CLAIRE: Okay then.

(Realizing she might have hurt CALVIN, ROSIE *slowly turns to him.)*

ROSIE: Or…I could give it some thought…

CALVIN: That's fine, Rosie. To tell you the truth, I'm relieved. I barely know what to do with myself, much less a teenaged girl.

CLAIRE: So I'm going to get my stuff and move in here with you. We'll have fun, I promise.

ROSIE: Are you still gonna teach?

CLAIRE: Yes. I am. With a few changes in the curriculum. A little Sartre wouldn't hurt. I might even convince them to let me direct *No Exit.*

CALVIN: Instead of *You're a Good Man, Charlie Brown?* Good luck with that.

CLAIRE: What about you, Calvin? You still wanna be a minister?

CALVIN: As long as they'll have me.

CLAIRE: Does that mean—you still have faith?

CALVIN: I think I do. Today helped a lot. Gave me a sense of purpose.

CLAIRE: Good. As long as people continue to die, you'll be happy in your job.

CALVIN: Let's hope. I also think I may get out there. Maybe even start dating.

ROSIE: Are you allowed to do that?

CALVIN: Yes, Presbyterian ministers are allowed.

CLAIRE: Did you feel that, Rosie? I think it was a disturbance in the force.

ROSIE: But not Catholic priests.

CALVIN: Correct.

CLAIRE: Unfortunately for you. That guy was cute.

CALVIN: Shut up Claire.

ROSIE: Wait a minute. Are you saying…you're…

CALVIN: No. *(Pause)* I'm not sure. Maybe.

CLAIRE: I see you've given this a lot of thought.

CALVIN: I'm kind of a late bloomer, okay? Besides, it's not like I've been able to do a lot of research. The average age of my parishioners is about seventy-three.

ROSIE: Eww.

CALVIN: Exactly. So tell you what. When this subject becomes relevant, you two will be the first to know.

ROSIE: But you think you can love God—and people too?

CALVIN: That's not a conflict, Rosie. Some people believe that's the best way to love God. John Calvin said that. And Jesus too. I should have reversed that.

ROSIE: So maybe I can still serve God … without being a nun?

CALVIN: Of course.

CLAIRE: Rosie. Are you saying…you might like to go on dates yourself?

ROSIE: Maybe.

CLAIRE: That's a great idea.

CALVIN: Which way are *you* leaning, Rosie? Because either way—

ROSIE: I like boys, Calvin. So shut up.

CLAIRE: Listen, sweetheart. I'd be lying to you if I said I knew the first thing about being a mother. I've never had kids of my own, and most of what I've observed from my peers has been pretty…horrifying. So I'm going to try and *not* learn from anything I've ever witnessed. But I love you, and I'll always tell you the truth and treat you like the young adult you are. And you can talk to me about anything. I mean *anything*. Without shame or embarassment.

ROSIE: Really?

CLAIRE: Really. Cross my heart.

ROSIE: Can you help me get birth control?

(CALVIN *flinches.* CLAIRE *freezes.*)

CALVIN: Ow. I just got whiplash.

CLAIRE: Well, um, we'll have to discuss this, Rosie. Is there…someone in particular?

ROSIE: Umm…

CLAIRE: No. You don't mean…

(ROSIE *giggles.*)

CLAIRE: Goddammit. That little creep.

CALVIN: Claire!

CLAIRE: Are you sure you don't want to be a nun?

END OF PLAY

9 7 9 8 8 8 8 5 6 0 1 9 8